The Family
Financial Book

A Guide to Understanding Every Day Money Matters and Improving Your Finances

Victor M. Carrion

The Family Financial Book

A Guide to Understanding Every Day Money Matters and Improving Your Finances

Copyright © 2017 Victor M. Carrion

Other Works By The Author

The Family Financial Book (due in 2018)

(Part Two)

Preface

This book was written to assist families with getting into good financial standing, and to equip them with basic financial knowledge and tools. They can take action today by setting up their finances to live a better life. I wanted this book to be a road map or a guide showing people how to take immediate action with their finances. We live in an era where things move fast and people want information they can apply immediately, so that was my intention in writing this book, it is short, simple, and to the point. Many friends have asked me to get together with them to discuss their finances; however, I don't have the time to talk to every friend or family member to share basic financial information so here in these pages are the basics to get you started.

What to Expect From This Book

In this simple financial book, you and your family will learn basic financial information as well as money consciousness giving you and your family the tools you need to be financially successful. Some of the things you will learn about are emergency accounts, investment accounts, buying stocks, buying a home, retirement accounts, college funds, assembling a team of professionals, and gaining the money consciousness to win. The main purpose of this book is to empower you with financial knowledge and actionable steps so that you can live a more fulfilled and peaceful life knowing that your finances are being taken care of. It is written in a way that covers the **what** to do, **why** you need to do it, and **how** to do it. Enjoy!

Dedication

I would like to dedicate this book to all of the unrepresented people who need financial guidance and who have at one point or another struggled financially because they did not have the necessary tools, information, or money available to protect themselves. You are my primary inspiration and reason for writing this book. I would also like to dedicate this book to my beautiful fianceé Yarubys D. Gonzalez for her support, patience, unconditional love, and for believing and sticking with me through tough times.

I love you Yarubys.

Thank you.

TABLE OF CONTENTS

Chapter One:
The Basics - Savings

Taking care of your financial life is taking care of your health, your family, and yourself now and in the future when you're old and cannot work to support yourself. If you take care of your finances today you can even help out your children with their future financial needs. Taking care of your finances is a way of saying "I love and respect myself, as well as my family." Let's get started. Here is one thing you should to do right away.

Create an **Emergency Account** immediately with a minimum of three months ideally six months of savings to cover living expenses and pay for emergency items. **Why?** Because the average time it takes to recuperate from misfortune is approximately one to six months. If you get into a big car accident the recuperation time is roughly one to three months, and surgery takes about three to six months recovery time. A big percentage of people's average monthly expenses range from $2000 to about $10,000 a month. Let's say that your monthly expenses are $3000 per month multiplied by three months gives you $9000 to use for an emergency. For example, let's say you get into a car accident, the funds can be used as a down payment for your new vehicle as well as paying for a rental car. Other emergencies like your car breaking down or someone trying to sue you are reasons you can use your emergency account. If you are living paycheck to paycheck you are one paycheck away from being homeless. Think about that! One paycheck away from being homeless. So if you have three to six months saved in an emergency account you can pick yourself up from challenges life throws your way and never have to put yourself nor your family in the tough situations of being homeless or begging other people for food or money, or losing your spouse. Yes, you heard me right, losing your spouse.

Statistics state that a huge percentage of divorces are due to some sort of financial reason. So if you take care of your finances you can always solve other relationship issues that may arise without money pressures. All relationships have arguments and disagreements but when your finances are in bad shape, you are living paycheck to paycheck, and are constantly working full time; one little argument can sometimes turn into a big argument because of the stress created by not being financially healthy. Now, if you and your spouse are financially in good health and you get into an argument, at least you don't have money stress, and can look at the argument for what it is. This allows you to have a different outlook on the issue, and perhaps a little more patience. I'm not saying money can fix all relationship problems; it just takes off some of the pressure. Furthermore, many divorces arise from lack of financial compatibility. Meaning, one person is a financial wreck and the other person in the relationship is good at finances or wants to better his or herself financially. Don't want to spend a lot of time talking about divorce here, however, I believe it's very important to include this fact since we are talking about family finances. I didn't mean to derail myself by speaking about divorces, so let's get back to your emergency account. **An emergency account is not an option** so please start your emergency account today. Many people ask me how much should I start putting in the emergency account? The answer is whatever you can afford, if you can only start with $20 or $30 dollars a month that's a good start. An ideal amount to start with your emergency account should be a minimum of $100 dollars, but if all you can do is $50 start with that. If you can afford to put more money into your emergency account every month, I encourage you to do it. Some people do not have an emergency account simply because they never heard of one, or they don't know why it's important to have one. Other people simply don't have an emergency account because they try to live like the Kardashians and attempt to buy things that make them look rich when in fact they are not. When you try to keep up with the Kardashians without having their wealth, you are only getting yourself into a bigger financial hole. To want luxurious things is healthy and good because we live in an abundant universe, however, how you go about acquiring those things is what matters. I'm writing a *Part Two* of the *Family Financial Book* that covers how to obtain all the luxurious things you want in a healthy and responsible manner. Now, if you are a person that likes to live modestly, that's healthy and good too. Luxury is not what makes you a good person; your values make you a good person. There is a great book called *The Millionaire Next Door written* by Thomas J. Stanley, Ph.D. and William D. Kano, Ph.D. that illustrates who the real wealthy are in the United States, and how modestly these rich people live. It covers what they buy, the stores where they shop, cars they drive, credit cards they use, and how they live in regular neighborhoods in modest homes. Some people may argue that they don't make enough money or that money is already too tight with what they currently make to save anything. This is how you fix that. Cut down on unnecessary expenses, like dining out, buying things you don't need, or cutting down on your Starbuck's visits. A grande size drink at Starbucks is approximately $5 dollars, multiply that times 4 (per month) equals $20 dollars. That's if you do this once a week, many people go there more than once a week. Other ways of coming up with the money is to do some over time work, get a part time job, sell things on the side temporarily until you fulfill at least your three month goal. Many successful people even save up to one full year of their monthly expenses.

Simple Steps to Creating an Emergency Savings Fund

First, start by writing down your monthly expenses, write your monthly expenses category on the left side of the paper and your monthly income on the right. Add all of your monthly expenses and write the total on the bottom of the page. Then, write down your monthly income on the same piece of paper including your pay, rental income, or any other source of income you may have. Last thing you want to do is to subtract your expenses from your income which equates the net amount of money you are left with. That's for budget purposes. The number you want to focus for this example is the total number of your **monthly expenses** multiplied by three or six months depending on how many months you want to include in your emergency account. Here is a chart to give you an example.

Monthly Bills	Company	Income	Company
$100.00	Charity	$4,500.00	Job
$1,350.00	Rent/Mortgage	$1,500.00	Rental Prop. #1
$150.00	Emergency Acct.	$1,300.00	Rental Prop. #2
$500.00	Food	$1,100.00	Stocks Dividend
$200.00	Gasoline	Total Income	
$150.00	Utilities	$8,400.00	

$65.00	Internet		
$55.00	Cell		
$75.00	Credit Card	Total Income	$8,400.00
$150.00	Entertainment	Total Expenses	- $2,795.00
Total Expenses		Total Savings	$5,605.00
$2,795.00	3 Month Reserves	6 Month Reserves	
	$8,385.00	$16,770.00	

Second, look at your emergency account as a **bill** that you have to pay every month. If you have a primary bank account open a separate bank account with a different institution and set up automatic payments through your primary bank account to your new bank account as a bill that needs to be paid using a free BillPay option that most banks provide. The reason for setting up your emergency account with a different bank is so that you won't have direct access to this money. **Never! I repeat never touch this money unless it is a real emergency** and if you follow this rule you will be in good shape. Here is a list of what constitutes an emergency:

- Loss of job: you need to continue paying rent and other bills.

- Car accident: you need money for medical expenses, a down payment for a new vehicle, and rental car fees to go to work until you find your new car.

- Surgery: you don't have sick leave and need to continue paying your monthly bills, as well as out of pocket medical expenses.

- Law suit: someone is trying to sue you and you need to get an attorney to protect yourself, or somebody wronged you and you are suing them.

- Funeral: someone in your family dies and you need money to help for funeral expenses.

- Illness: you or someone in your family have a chronic disease and need to use the funds to assist with the medical expenses.

You can refer to this list of reasons to use your emergency account; however, you are more than welcome to make your own list.

Get into the habit of setting up automatic payments one time, and then you can forget about them. This way you'll never miss a payment. This also gives you more time to spend with family or work on other projects. All you have to do is set up a separate bank account, call your current bank to ask them if they provide free bill pay service which most banks do, and ask your bank how to set it up. It's that easy. Now that we talked about how to protect ourselves from challenges let's talk about how to build our wealth.

Chapter Two:
Making Money Work for You
- Investments

In order to win at the game of money we need to treat money as a game that we can play; this takes away all the stress, and lets you focus on the game. The reason we want to look at money as a game is to get rid of all the tension and fear which can prevent us from making lots of money, cause us to lose money, and miss out on great opportunities. In the last chapter we spoke about protecting ourselves from misfortunes, in this chapter we will focus on building wealth by investing money and putting it to work for us. Once you establish your emergency account or responsible account which is what I like to call it, you can then start your investing. There are lots of things you can invest your money in, but we will focus on stocks and real estate in this chapter as these are the most common types of investments and the easiest ones to get into.

Before you open your investment account you want to have at least two months saved up in your emergency account, so that when an emergency occurs you won't take your money out of your investment account. **Note! Make sure that when you open your investment account you don't stop paying your emergency account bill.** You're probably wondering how you should allocate your money between your emergency account and your investment account. Here is a rule of thumb on how to allocate your money. This is kind of a personal thing, but if you want some idea here it is; I like to use the 70/30 rule, meaning, I put 70% towards my investment account and 30% towards my emergency account. If you want to be more conservative you can do 50/50. This only applies after you have **at least two months** of expenses saved in your emergency account. I do it this way because although it's important to protect yourself and your family from an emergency, you also need to make money, which creates more assets which give you passive income (income that you don't have to work for) and in return allow you to put more money into your emergency and investment accounts. This is another way of protecting yourself and your family. Now, once you reach your goal of six months of expenses in your emergency account you can put 100% of your money into your investment account or other investment projects you may have.

Why do you need to invest your money? Because you are only one person, and there are only 24 hours in a day. Therefore, you need your money to work for you when you cannot because you don't have the time to do five jobs to reach your goals, so investing is a great tool to assist you in reaching your financial goals. It's almost like creating another you. You can only do so much overtime in a day. You don't want to work yourself to death either. It's good and healthy to work long hours, but you have to work smart not hard, and that is why we create an investment account. In this section I will cover what you need to know in order to invest your money without high risk. Before I dive into the different types of investments I would like to cover one quick point here about investing, and that is you don't need lots of money to invest. You need some knowledge and information in order for you to achieve your goals, which requires you to do about two hours of research daily and or study the subject that you want to learn. I spend at least two hours sometimes up to five hours or more daily to find the knowledge I'm seeking. If you want to get there quicker and avoid costly mistakes get yourself a mentor to help you out, read books, and attend seminars. People often sound comedic to me when they say I'm going to invest in real estate or stocks and become rich without knowing what the heck they're doing when they start. In order for you to become rich in these areas you have to know what you are doing, in other words, know your trade. Understand that real estate or stocks for example should be treated as **careers** if you want to make it big in these two areas. I just want to be honest with you regarding investments and tell you about doing your homework before you invest. One great book that illustrates this point is *The Richest Man In Babylon* by George Clason . "Gold slippeth away from the man who invests it in businesses or purposes with which he is not familiar or which are not approved by those skilled in its keep". Do not panic! I will give you investment basics in stocks, and the steps to buy your house without you having to become a financial guru. Let's dive into some of the different types of investments you can get into.

Buying Stocks

What is a stock? **A stock** is a share in the ownership of a company. Stock represents a claim on the company's assets and earnings. As you acquire more stock, your ownership stake in the company becomes greater. How are stocks created? Stocks are created when a company decides to "go public", which means selling a chunk of the company to public investors in the form of a stock. When you buy a stock you are actually part owners of companies like Apple, Google, or Tesla. When you invest your money in stocks, you buy shares of a stock in that particular company. The beauty of buying a stock is that you can own a portion of a business without having to run the operations of a business, such as, customer service, payroll, taxes, operations, and finance. You reap the benefits of a company's growth by simply owning shares of a company. It's that easy! On top of that you get paid a **dividend yield**, which means you get money deposited into your brokerage account on a quarterly basis (every 3 months) or in some cases every month by simply being a share owner of a company. Keep in mind that not all companies pay a dividend, so buy the ones that do pay a dividend. A dividend is similar to having a CD (Certificate of Deposit) account at a bank that pays you interest for having your money parked with a bank. This is a form of collecting passive income. **Passive income** basically means collecting money without having to work for it. You basically do the work in the beginning by setting up your assets and then you collect passive income without having to work. Here is a list of some assets that pay you a passive income:

1. Rental Income Properties.
2. Stocks that pay a dividend.
3. Businesses that pay you passive income.
4. Books/Songs you collect royalties when someone buys books or songs you wrote.
5. Options investing, you can do Covered Calls which is a conservative approach to receiving money on a monthly basis.

Steps to Selecting Stocks

There are a couple of things you need to know when buying a stock. First, you need to know **fundamental analysis**, which is a method of evaluating a security in an attempt to measure its intrinsic value (actual value of a company) by looking at the company's financials. This will tell you what stock to buy. You need to understand the financial status of a company to know that you are buying a financially sound company at a bargain.

Market capitalization is a very important thing to look at when conducting your fundamental analysis, which is the value of company's stock. This figure is found by taking the stock price and multiplying it by the total number of shares outstanding (total number of shares). The bigger the company the less likely it will go bankrupt so you might want to start out with **large cap** companies which have a market cap from $10 billion to $200 billion or **mega-cap** companies which have a market cap of $200 billion or greater. But this is not to say that big companies never go bankrupt, some big companies have in the past like the **Enron** scandal who filed for Chapter 11 bankruptcy on December 2, 2001.

Earnings -You want to look at these because without earnings a company can fall and die. Look at the company's earnings for the last ten years or at least the last five years. This will let you know whether the company has been increasing or decreasing their earnings. Some years earnings may go up and in other years earnings may go down. If the company's earnings have been going up in the last ten years chances are the company's earnings will continue to go up. **P/E ratio or Price to Earnings ratio** is another thing you want to look at, P/E ratio will tell you whether you are buying stock of a company at a bargain or you are over paying for a stock. The formula for the price to earnings ratio is very simple: you divide the stock price by the yearly earnings and this will give you a ratio. As a rule of thumb a high P/E ratio would be from 18 to 25 or higher. Fair price of a company would be approximately from 13 to 16. And, a discounted P/E ratio would be consider 12 or below. Anything in the single digits you are getting a great bargain. A higher ratio equates to a high priced or overpriced stock. And, a lower ratio equates a bargain. It's important to take into account that some companies under certain sectors or industries might have a high P/E ratio from 18-28 and that may be normal for certain companies. Although the P/E ratio is one of the most important elements to look for when shopping for a bargain when buying a stock company you may want to look at the forward P/E ratio as well. The forward P/E ratio is a future estimate of a company's earnings. If a **forward P/E ratio** is less than the current P/E ratio, that means that the company's future earnings projection will be higher making the stock more valuable.

Total Cash and Total Debt: You might want to look at how much cash and debt the company has. If the company has too much debt that means that the company has poor management skills and may suffer down the road. **Total Debt** - this is how much the company owes. The maximum debt a company should have is approximately no more than thirty three percent of the market cap. **Total Cash**- this is how much liquid money the company has on its books; the more cash the the company has the better because this allows the company to make mistakes and be able to recuperate from them. A good number to have in cash is one billion or more. Here is an example of a great company with good financials, Apple, Inc. Apple is a company that has great financials and have been continuously growing for years. They are sitting on lots of cash and have very little debt. And, their earnings and dividend yield have been continually increasing. Not trying to promote Apple here, I'm just using them as an example of a good company with strong financials. I'm not telling you to go out and buy Apple stock; just because the company has good financials doesn't mean that you are buying this company at a bargain. To determine whether you are buying a company at a discount or not check out their P/E ratio along with other fundamentals included in this book. Start with **large cap** or **mega cap** companies. The name of the game is to buy big financially sound companies at a **discount**. A good place to start is by subscribing to IBD *Investment Business Daily* which is a financial newspaper that provides you with decent stock picks, however, you have to do your fundamental analysis before you buy. Another thing you can do to find good stocks is to use the search tab provided by your brokerage company. By inputting a search criteria you will get a list of stocks to consider. Do not rely on what anybody tells you to buy; let the numbers of the company tell you what to buy. If you are new to the game stick to large companies and buy them at a discount. That is the safest way to do it. This may sound like some complicated or boring stuff to you, but it's easier than you think. If you would like to know more about fundamental analysis here is a list of books you might find interesting:

One Up On Wall Street by Peter Lynch and John Rothchild

The Intelligent Investor by Benjamin Graham

Learn to Earn by Peter Lynch and John Rothchild.

How to Do Fundamental Analysis

Go to www.yahoofinance.com and key in a company name or ticker symbol on the search tab and then click on the **statistics tab**, and that will give you a good gauge of the company's fundamentals. It will give you all the numbers on the financials, like the P/E ratio, market cap, debt, cash, dividend, revenue, and other pertinent financial information of a company. It's that simple. There are other awesome tabs you can look at that Yahoo Finance offers, such as, holders, financials, analyst, and many other great tools. Be sure to check them all out, its free information. Furthermore, you can use all the amazing tools that your brokerage company offers, such as, a fundamental analysis page, and the financial page. Also, take advantage of all the educational videos, webinars, and charts to see the volume and trends of a company. In order for you to be able to read charts that cover trends, volume, and other technical indicators it's important to know technical analysis. **Technical analysis** is basically the examination of past historical price movements to forecast future financial price movements. I go in depth on fundamental analysis, technical analysis, and public sentiment on another book that I'm currently writing which focuses just on stocks (due in 2018). Talking about stocks in full requires lots of information and is outside the scope of this book. Next let's talk about brokerage accounts.

Opening a Brokerage Account

In order for you to invest in stocks you will need to open a brokerage account. What is a brokerage account? A brokerage account is an arrangement between an investor and a licensed brokerage firm that allows the investor to deposit funds and place investment orders through the brokerage. The next step after opening your brokerage account is to transfer money from your bank account into your brokerage account so that you can start investing. Your money needs to be in your brokerage account to be able to invest. I have included a list of some of the most popular brokerage firms so that you can start investing right away. There are many more brokerage companies out there that you can pick from, however, I just wanted to give you a place to start.

TDAmeritrade	Charles Schwab	E-Trade
www.tdameritrade.com	www.schawb.com	www.etrade.com
1-800-454-9272	1800-435-4000	1-888-639-4353

No minimum deposit	$1000 minimum deposit	No minimum deposit
Trading Fee: $6.95	Trading Fee: $4.95	Trading Fee: $6.95

How to Place an Order

Placing your order: is when you place an order to buy stock. You can easily do it yourself from your laptop, or computer by keying in a ticker symbol, price you want to pay, and the amount of shares you want to buy. The other way is to use your phone by calling your brokerage company so that they can place the order for you and you pay a higher fee. If you do it yourself you save money on the transaction fee by only paying between $4.95 to about $9 dollars. If you call your brokerage company to do it for you the fee will be between $25 to $30 dollars per transaction. Yes, there are some small fees when buying stocks. There are a few different types of orders; however, I will talk about the two most common types of orders. First is a **market order**, which means you buy a stock at the current market price or the next available price closest to the market price. Then we have a **limit order**, which means you state the price you want to pay for the stock. In other words, I will pay this price or better. For example, let's say you are buying Microsoft (MSFT) which is currently selling for $74 and you want to pay $73, so you put a limit order of $73 dollars per share. If the price for Microsoft drops to your limit of $73 or less your order will get filled, if the market doesn't reach $73 your order won't get filled. When placing your order you will need to indicate how long you want your order to last. Here are a couple of options: you have the daily, which means your order will expire by the end of the day, and you have the **GTC Good Till Cancelled,** which usually expires within three months. The reason you set a time frame is so that you can place your order and do other things without having to be glued to your computer waiting for your desired price to hit. You simply set up your terms and go about your day. It's that simple. As I mentioned earlier I will write a separate book just about stocks and will go over all the different strategies and advanced order types. This portion of the book is to give you the basics so that you can take action to get started in buying stocks. When selling stocks you basically apply the same order types and time frames mentioned above. When should I sell my stock? If you bought a good stock company at a discount and are collecting a good dividend yield you don't have to sell your stock. Simply continue to collect your dividend to buy more shares of that stock. A good time to sell a stock is after making your desired profit and finding a better stock deal than the one you have.

Buying a Home

Buying a home is a process that many people dread; however, I will include some important information and tips for buying a home to make things easier for you. **Why** should I buy a home? For starters you need a roof over your head, and this can be accomplished through owning a home or renting. What's a better choice? When you buy a home your monthly mortgage payments go towards paying off your house, whereas, when you pay rent your money is going down the drain. Now, if the housing market is inflated (properties are overpriced), then renting may be a better option. Let's begin talking about the home buying process. First, is the **financing** part, know your credit score and have a copy of your credit report if possible. You can obtain a free copy of your credit report once a year through www.annualcreditreport.com. The reason you need your credit report is to know if there is any derogatory information that can affect your credit score and also to assist your loan officer in pre-qualifying you. You will need your last two years of W-2's, or 1099's if you are self employed, three to six months of bank statements, and your last two pay stubs from work. These are the primary things you will be asked for when buying a home so have them ready. You may also need other things if you are refinancing your house like your mortgage statement, home insurance, and your warranty deed. Where can I find a loan officer? A good place to start would be to go the institution where you do your banking because you already have a business relationship which can make the process much easier. I really like credit unions and community banks because they offer low financing fees. Here are some guidelines regarding how much banks are willing to lend you when buying a house. **Primary residence** between 95% to 100%, FHA loans 96.5%, conventional loans can be 95%, and VA loans all the way up to 100% (no money down) on primary residences only. VA loans are offered to people that have served or are currently enrolled in the military. On **vacation homes** you can find conventional loans that range between 90% to 95%. In order to qualify for a **vacation home/second home,** your vacation home must be 100 miles away from your primary residence and should be occupied for 14 days out of a year. The amount a bank loans on **investment properties** is usually 80% of the property's value.

Buying a home and renting it out is an excellent form of passive income which has great tax benefits as well. You can deduct many rental property expenses when doing your taxes. Once you provide your loan officer with your prequalifying documents, ask him or her how much money you qualify for to buy a house. This will give you and your realtor an idea what price range you are looking for and what type of home you are looking for. Some places to look for realtors are www.zillow.com, www.realtor.com, and www.trulia.com. Once you have your financing in place you can then start to look for homes. Let's say you find a home you like and would like to make an offer on that property. Have your realtor draw up an offer for you and if you choose you can always have a real estate attorney review it for extra peace of mind. Now, you don't have to go through an attorney that is something optional. Let's say that your offer is accepted and you and the seller agree to the terms and conditions. Make sure that you inspect the home thoroughly with a professional home inspector during your **inspection period** which is usually within the first 5 to 15 days of an executed contract (sales contract signed by all parties). If you are happy with the results of the inspection and the home, the last thing will be your closing. You can elect to close with an attorney of choice or a title company which is any institution qualified to issue title insurance which also handles all the closing legalities pertaining to a real estate deal. This is the place where the buyer and seller meet with a closing agent to sign the final closing documents, and where monies are distributed electronically or by check to all parties involved. Now that we've covered investing in stocks and buying a home, let's talk about planning for our future.

Chapter Three:
Planning for the Future – Retirement Accounts, Prenuptial Agreements, College Savings Accounts

Retirement Accounts

In order for us to plan for our future we need to take actionable steps during our youth. And, what better than the book of *Proverbs* of *The Bible* to illustrate this concept. Proverbs 6:6 states, "Go to the ant (learn from the ant), O sluggard (you lazy person), Observe her ways and be wise (model her ways and you too will be wise), 6:7 Which, having no chief, Officer or ruler (which takes action on her own), 6:8 Prepares her food in the **summer** And gathers her provision in the harvest (prepare during your youth to receive the benefits when you are old)." The key word in proverbs 6:8

is summer which is referring to our youth. Now that we've covered taking action during our youth, we can now jump into retirement accounts. People often get confused with what retirement accounts are and how they work. I would like to start this section by getting rid of all the confusion people may have regarding retirement accounts. For starters retirement accounts like a 401(k), 457 plan, 403(b), or an Individual Retirement Account (IRA) are all retirement accounts. That's the key, they are all retirement accounts with similar functions. You can pretty much do the same things with the 401(k), 457 plan, 403(b) or an IRA, the only difference is the investment options each retirement account may have. Meaning, some retirement accounts can invest in certain mutual fund companies and other retirement accounts can invest in other mutual fund companies. Also, the other difference is that some retirement accounts may offer tax advantages that other retirement accounts may not offer. For example, one tax benefit a 457 account has is that once you separate from your employer you can take your funds out without having to pay a 10% penalty for early withdrawal (before your retirement age). These accounts still have to pay federal taxes like the others. **457 accounts** are usually offered to **government** or **state** employees. And, **403(b)** accounts are offered to employees of various non-profit organizations such as schools and other tax-exempt organizations that can benefit from enrolling in a 403(b) plan, officially known as a tax-deferred annuity. The 403(b) accounts are very common among public school teachers and other staff members. 401(k) **Plan** - is a contribution plan usually sponsored by **a private sector employer** which are commonly found among every day businesses and corporations. Now if your employer offers neither the 401(k), 403(b), nor a 457 plan you can always open an IRA with a bank or a brokerage firm. An IRA is very similar to a 401(k) and sometimes may have more flexibility as far as investment options. The current contribution amounts for an **IRA** are $5,500, or

$6,500 if 50 or older per year, whereas, a 401(k), 403(b), and a 457 plan the contribution amounts are $18,000, or $24,000 if 50 or older per year. Banks and brokerage firms offer various investment options for an IRA, whereas if you have a 401(k) with your employer, you may be limited with the investment options often in the form of mutual funds. So, what is a mutual fund? A **mutual fund** is an investment security that enables investors to pool their money into one professionally managed investment. It's kind of like a salad, where the toppings are stocks, bonds, cash or a blend of stocks and bonds combined for one mutual fund portfolio. The difference between buying a stock and buying a mutual fund is that when you buy a stock you are buying one single company and when you invest in a mutual fund you are buying multiple companies and industries combined into one fund. People invest in mutual funds because they offer more safety due to diversification. You may be asking yourself should I invest in stocks or mutual funds? The answer is they are both good investment vehicles; however, between me and you the real money is made on individual stocks not mutual funds. If you don't believe me ask Warren Buffet. I will use billionaire Warren Buffet, one of the greatest stock investors of all time, to go over this example. Mr. Buffet invests in businesses which are individual stock companies, he then created Berkshire Hathaway, Inc. which is a form of a mutual fund because it contains a bunch of different stock companies that he bought individually and combined them into one fund to sell to the public. So here we have a billionaire and probably the number one stock investor in the world that invests his money into individual stock companies, takes these companies and creates his own mutual fund, which then sells to the public. That should tell you something. Berkshire Hathaway is more of an **ETF or exchange traded fund**. An exchange traded fund is basically a mutual fund that trades like a stock. Meaning, that you can buy or sell an ETF within the same day, whereas, with a mutual fund the transaction will go through on the next business day. Now, if you are just starting out and don't know about stocks, mutual funds are a great way to start and also a very good investment vehicle. I would like to point out that there are some good mutual funds that provide good returns on your investment. Now that we know how retirement accounts work, let's talk about how much money we should allocate into our retirement accounts. The ideal amount should be 10 percent of your gross monthly income. For example, let's say you make $60,000 annually divide that by 12 months in a year and multiply that by 10%. It should look like this: $60,000/12=$5,000 x 10%=$500 per month that should go into your retirement account. **You must learn to pay yourself first.** You are the most important person in the world, so please pay yourself first. On one of my favorite books called *The Richest Man In Babylon* by George Clason, states "Gold cometh gladly and in increasing quantity to any man who will put by not less than one-tenth of his earnings to create an estate for his future and that of his family". Now that we covered how much money you need to allocate to your retirement account, let's talk about setting up retirement accounts. There are two options when setting up retirement accounts:

1. **Pre-tax/Traditional account** simply means that pre-tax dollars will go into your retirement account. Your income will be taxed when you withdraw your money in the future at whatever tax bracket you may be in at that time. The first benefit is that it lowers your taxable income, for example, let's say you make $100,000 a year and you contributed $20,000 to your retirement account for that year, when you do your income taxes you will only pay taxes on the $80,000. The second benefit is that you can invest money which the government has not taxed. The third benefit is that you do not pay capital gains tax on your money every time you buy or sell because you are

investing from your retirement account which allows a break from capital gains tax.

2. **Roth account** is one where your taxed dollars go into your investment account, so you don't pay taxes in the future when you withdraw your money. The first benefit is that you are taxed up front and don't have to worry about being taxed later on. Taxes have cycles that go up and down, historically taxes have been going up since the year 1940. Will the tax bracket continue to go up in the future no one knows, all we know is that history usually repeats itself. Or to put it in the words of Mark Twain, "history doesn't often repeat itself but it often rhymes." You also have the same capital gains benefit of a traditional account.

Note! If your employer offers a matching benefit (where the company pays/matches your contribution) on a 401(k) or a 457 make sure you take advantage of this free

money. You can always open up both a traditional account and a roth account if you choose. If your employer offers neither, open an IRA with a bank or brokerage firm and be done. **The information contained here is meant for informational purposes only, you are advised to seek a tax professional in your state to go over tax rules and benefits that apply to your retirement account.**

Prenuptial Agreements

Since we are on the subject of planning for the future we might as well include prenuptial agreements if you are planning on getting married. Marriage is a beautiful experience and when people get married people usually get married for love and with the intention of staying in that relationship forever, however, not all relationships last forever. People do end up getting divorces. A **prenup** is a simple contract created before you get married stating how assets will be divided including, real estate, businesses, retirement accounts, cars, paintings, and bank accounts in case you get a divorce. You can even waive alimony or spouse support in most states. This is a list of some of the most common things included in a prenup, however, you can include any other type of asset you may have. Some things that **cannot** be include in a prenup are child support or child custody issues. The court has the final say in calculating child support. A court would not uphold a provision of a prenuptial agreement that dealt with child support, child custody, or visitation, because these are issues of **public policy**. Look at a prenup as a form of **insurance** in case the relationship doesn't work. Can I set up a prenup after marriage? Yes, you definitely can get a prenup after marriage. This contract, is known as a **post-nuptial agreement**, is drafted after marriage by those who are still married and either are contemplating separation or divorce or simply want to protect themselves for the unexpected in the future, according to the Legal Dictionary. Divorces are not a pretty thing, and if you don't have a prenup they can get very nasty. It's a lot easier to prepare a prenup than to go through a divorce without a prenup. Do not be afraid to speak to your fiance or fiancee' in regards to a prenup. It's like Tina Turner says, "what's love got to do with it!" Money and love are two separate things, so its ok to request a prenup. So, how do you set up a prenup? You can either do it your self or hire an attorney. To do it yourself you can use Nolo Press by going to www.nolo.com which has legal forms and a book on how to set up a prenup. To hire an attorney simply Google a **prenup attorney** near you or your zip code and you will find lots of attorneys willing to prepare a prenup for you. The fees can range from $800 to $1500 dollars in California where I currently reside. Other states may have lower or higher attorney fees depending on the state. Prenups can be created in just a couple of days. Once you have your prenup created by your attorney your spouse takes the prenup for a review with their attorney. Your spouse's attorney goes over the contract for a small fee of about $500 dollars and signs it. Once both attorneys sign the contract you and your spouse sign the contract in the presence of any public notary, which makes it official and legally binding. It's that simple! Children usually comes after marriage, so let's talk about preparing for our children's future education.

College Fund Accounts

It's a lot easier to put a little money away for your children's college education when they're young, than to come up with large amounts of money when they're grown and ready to start college. This brings me to the next topic which covers your children's college needs by opening a college fund. A **529 College Savings Plan** is one of the best secrets out there because you can put money towards your children's college expenses without the government taxing your accumulated invested earnings. It's an investment account to help your children with their college expenses. Your children can use the funds without having to pay any taxes on the funds. Please check with your tax specialist in your state, each state may have different tax laws. It doesn't get any better than this, you help your children with their college education and the government doesn't tax the gains on your account. How awesome is that? You may be saying, I'm not sure I want to give my money to my children for their education, they can work to pay for their own education. That's fine if you feel that way, you might be barely getting by financially. Another way to look at it if you are doing financially well, is you have to give your money to the government via taxes whether you want to or not, wouldn't you rather give some of your money towards your children's college education? I just think it makes more sense. Ask your benefit specialist if they offer 529 accounts and how to set it up. Here are some websites along with contact phone numbers of reputable companies to open up a 529 plan in all fifty states just in case your employer doesn't offer a 529 plan.

www.merrilledge.com/open-account/college-savings 1-888-637-3343

www.troweprice.com/College-Savings 1-800-369-3641

https://investor.vanguard.com/529-plan/open-account 1-866-734-4533

Chapter Four:
Getting your Team Together
– Advisors, Attorneys,
Accountants

Building wealth is a team sport, therefore, you will need a group of professionals on your team. Please don't try to do it all on your own because you will waste lots of time and remember that time equals money. Just when you think you are saving money what you're really doing is wasting it. Instead of focusing on making money by doing the things you are good at you are wasting your time in attempting to do things that you are not specialized in. I'll give you my example with this book you are reading. I wrote everything in this book myself, however, I hired a graphic designer to do the front/back cover and a professional editor to edit/proofread my book. It would have been a waste of my time for me to try to do the art when I didn't go to school for that, or attempt to edit my book when I can hire a professional editor for an expert opinion at a very reasonable cost. In addition, I hired a self-publishing company that walks you through the process of creating your ebook and lists your book for you with companies like Amazon, iBooks, Barnes and Noble, and others. Instead of wasting my time with things I'm not good at I'd rather be making money doing the things I know how to do like investing, running my online business, and writing more books. Here is a list of professionals you need on your team:

- a good contract attorney, tax attorney,
- a good CPA (Certified Public Accountant) for your taxes,
- a good financial planner,

Your job is to spend some time doing the research to find the Michael Jordan's for the professions mentioned above, meaning, the best in their field.

What you do is Google a list of the professionals mentioned above in your area, and set up a free consultation appointment. Write down your questions before you go, this way you don't waste the professional's time and both of you come out winning from the meeting. Ask straight forward questions and avoid all the excessive narrative. Be prepared and do not waste people's time expecting them to tell you everything. It's your job to ask the right questions, at the end of the day people don't really care and shouldn't have to care whether you got the information you were seeking or not. It's your responsibility! I don't mean to sound harsh here, but this is a form of tough love to help you out so that you have a positive experience when contacting and dealing with professionals. When dealing with attorneys don't be intimidated by them, they are people just like you and me and the more you interview attorneys the more knowledge you'll gain. Also, you may want to contact bar associations, better business bureaus etc. to check on pros you are considering. Follow your gut instincts to pick a good professional. This is something that I've learned by reading some of

Donald Trump's books, like the *Art of the Deal,* and *Think Big and Kick Ass* which was co-authored with Bill Zanker of the Learning Annex. I want to thank Mr. Trump for sharing his valuable knowledge without sugar coating things. Also, I'm extremely thankful to Mr. Bill Zanker for creating the Learning Annex, an event where top notch motivational speakers, financial gurus, hypnotists, spiritual leaders, etc. teach and educate people. I remember attending the Learning Annex back in October 2006 in New York at the Jacobs and Javits Convention Center. Some of the key speakers that night were Donald Trump, Tony Robbins, Marshall Silver, Robert and Kim Kiyosaki, Jay Mitton, and many more amazing speakers that changed my life forever. After attending that two day weekend my life has never been the same. I would like to express my deepest gratitude to Bill Zanker for making it possible for everyone to be able to attend this life changing phenomenal educational experience at the Learning Annex.

Chapter Five:
The Winning Mind Set

In this chapter I will talk about how your subconscious mind affects your ability to acquire money and other material possessions. If you have been conditioned to think in impoverished or mediocre ways, chances are that's the kind of material reality you will have. Even if you want to be rich until you fix your mental programming it's going to be very hard and almost impossible for you to be rich. Let me explain why. We have two minds that have different functions and act in different ways. First, we have the **conscious mind** which is the mind that thinks and reasons. That's the mind that determines whether what I'm telling you right now is bullshit or not. Second, we have the **subconscious mind** which operates 24/7; it never stops working even in your sleep. The mind that controls us about 95 percent of the time is our subconscious mind, as a result, even if your conscious mind says I want to be rich, but your subconscious mind is conditioned to think in mediocre ways, chances are you will never be rich. According to Dr. Bruce Lipton Ph.D. and other neuroscientists show that "most of your decisions, actions, emotions and behavior depend on the 95 percent of brain activity that is beyond your conscious awareness, which means that 95 to 99 percent of your behavior comes from the programming in your subconscious mind." Many successful people understand this concept and have used different methods to reprogram their subconscious mind. Now that we know that the subconscious mind controls our physical reality not just with money but with everything in life, let's work on reprogramming the subconscious mind. Why try to do all the heavy lifting with your conscious mind when you can have your subconscious mind do it by creating the right opportunities, attracting the right people into your life, and by attracting the right knowledge. I will include some tools for you to accomplish the task of reprogramming your subconscious mind into wealth consciousness to attract the life you always wanted and deserve. Let's begin with **autosuggestion**, which is using affirmations to speak to yourself; speaking to yourself in the present moment will create powerful results. Start by creating a list of the words "I AM" X, and replace X with whatever you want to be. For example, I am confident, I am attractive, I am a money magnet, etc.... Read this list out loud once in the morning and once before retiring to bed. The reason for this is because when you awaken you are in a hypnotic state and your subconscious mind is more receptive to suggestion and at night because it is the last information you hear before retiring to bed, which allows the information to go directly into your subconscious mind. A great book I recommend that covers autosuggestion and self confidence is *Think and Grow Rich* written by Napoleon Hill. This book includes thirteen wealth principles to achieve wealth and success. An amazing book! It takes approximately twenty-one to thirty days to reprogram your subconscious mind. If you want more profound results do this in front of a mirror and say your I AM affirmations out loud and add emotional feeling to them. **Visualization** is another form of reprogramming your subconscious mind, which should be performed for thirty minutes daily. You simply visualize yourself in the future as the person you intend to be and see how peaceful your face looks, your calm body language, how powerful, wealthy, healthy, and relaxed you are. This will attract the opportunities to be that self you always dreamed of being, and one which you might be afraid of seeing because you are afraid it might never happen. I'm here to tell you that if you do your part, you will become that person you always dreamed about. I'm also here to tell you that if you don't do your part you will never become that person. Here is some homework for you to do, write down your perfect day of work and your perfect day of play and read it out loud every day. This is another way of visualizing your ideal self. If you follow all the exercises here you will wake up one day as that person you always wanted to be. **Repetition, repetition, repetition** is the key to success in becoming who you want to be. The million dollar question is, are you willing to pay the price for your dreams? The price is not that costly, however, you must repeat this process on a daily basis and never ever stop applying the tools. That's the price! What makes the price difficult is that you are saying and imagining things that you are currently not. That could be a disgusting feeling! Don't worry about that, even if it makes you feel uncomfortable. Doing things wrong for many years is going to feel right, and doing things right is going to feel wrong, or at least different. That's normal, but don't let it stop you. Keep on through repetition until you plant the seed into your subconscious mind. Your subconscious mind in return will help you with the rest. The feeling of being uncomfortable could be painful, however, it helps you grow spiritually, mentally, emotionally, and financially. Feeling uncomfortable is what makes people throw in the towel and quit, that is why these people will never get to the top. And, then they have the nerve to say things like this stuff doesn't work or the Law of Attraction doesn't work and blame everything but themselves. Just like the losers that say stocks, real estate, options, and businesses don't work. The truth of the matter is that you are the one who doesn't work because you want something for nothing and that's not how it works. Just like the people that want their money to grow first and then they want to grow later. It works the other way around, you must grow first and then your money will grow. I learned in a great book that covers the psychology of investing called *Trading in the Zone* by Mark Douglas that one of the biggest fears people have besides public speaking, or dying in burning fire is the fear of being wrong. This is a one of the main reasons why so many brilliant and talented people fail at investing in stocks. I bring this point up to make you aware that people will try things for one week or a month and say "oh that didn't work." It's a lot easier to blame something or someone else for your failures. It kind of minimizes the pain, however, that's a loser's mentality! Take responsibility for your failures and don't blame the government, your parents, nor the economy. Blame yourself! The more honest you are with yourself the faster you will reach financial success. **Note! You have to be extremely honest with yourself even if it's painful.** Robert Kiyosaki, in the book *The Business School*, states that when learning about investment or something new you want to get good at you need to give yourself at least five years to learn it well. Let's get back to the imagination to wrap things up. Albert Einstein said, "Imagination is more powerful than knowledge," so use your imagination wisely. Do not imagine negative things because you will attract those thoughts too. Remember that the subconscious mind just feeds back to you what you feed it through your conscious mind. **Hypnosis** is another great tool to use for reprogramming the subconscious mind; it's basically relaxing your conscious mind to allow suggestions to penetrate your subconscious mind. Many people think hypnosis is something taboo or occult when it's really not. You are conditioned on a daily basis through television, politicians, and people that tell you something which you believe, as a result, it becomes your psychological, emotional, and physical reality. Another important step, is **meditation** or **prayer,** use some type of meditation or prayer to cleanse yourself daily from anger and negative thoughts to allow blessings to enter into your life. Get rid of your anger by forgiving those who have wronged you, don't do it for them, do it for yourself. Anger and negative thoughts are what keep blessings from entering into your life. Remember that when you don't forgive someone you are giving your power away to the people that have wronged you and they don't deserve that. Also, forgive yourself for your mistakes.

Conclusion

I hope this book gives you the direction and knowledge to get you started in achieving financial stability. Remember that each financial tool described in this book has a different role, and should be treated separately. For example, the emergency account is designed to protect you from unforeseeable hardships, the retirement account is to support you through your golden years, and your investment account is designed so that your money can grow as a form of passive income. Make it a goal to have your house and your cars paid off by the time you retire or at least close to paying it off. You shouldn't have money worries when you retire if you follow the easy steps laid out for you in this book. Retirement should be a time when you enjoy your family, grandchildren, and get to travel to places you always wanted to see. In order to reach levels of success ask for help, forgive yourself and others, have compassion and love for every soul whether it is in human form or not, give when you can and be open to receive, form good habits and never deviate from them. When you find information that's valuable take **immediate action** by applying the knowledge you've gained. Remember, that knowledge is only potential power, continual action on your knowledge is real power. This book was written to give every family an idea of how to structure their finances and establish the appropriate money mind set. It was written with love and with the hopes that everyone can live a high quality and peaceful life. Thank you.

Reference List

The Millionaire Next Door written by Thomas J. Stanley, Ph.D. and William D. Kano, Ph.D.

The Richest Man In Babylon by George Clason . "Gold slippeth away from the man who invests it in businesses or purposes with which he is not familiar or which are not approved by those skilled in its keep".

IBD *Investment Business Daily (Financial Newspaper)*

One Up On Wall Street by Peter Lynch and John Rothchild

The Intelligent Investor by Benjamin Graham

Learn to Earn by Peter Lynch and John Rothchild.

The Family Financial Book (Part Two) by Victor M. Carrion

The Bible, Proverbs 6:6 states, "Go to the ant (learn from the ant), O sluggard (you lazy person), Observe her ways and be wise (model her ways and you too will be wise), 6:7 Which, having no chief, Officer or ruler (which takes action on her own), 6:8 Prepares her food in the **summer** And gathers her provision in the harvest (prepare during your youth to receive the benefits when you are old)."

The Richest Man In Babylon by George Clason, states "Gold cometh gladly and in increasing quantity to any man who will put by not less than one-tenth of his earnings to create an estate for his future and that of his family"

Art of the Deal by Donald J. Trump

Think Big and Kick Ass by Donald J. Trump & Bill Zanker of the Learning Annex

Think and Grow Rich by Napoleon Hill

Trading in the Zone by Mark Douglas

The Business School by Robert Kiyosaki